The Boys on Their Bony M

The Boys on Their Bony Mules

Poems by Miller Williams

Louisiana State University Press
Baton Rouge and London 1983

Copyright © 1983 by Miller Williams
All rights reserved
Manufactured in the United States of America
Designer: Joanna Hill
Typeface: Linotron Palatino
Typesetter: Graphic Composition Inc.
Printer: Thomson-Shore
Binder: John Dekker & Sons

Thanks are offered to the editors of the following magazines, in which some of the
poems in this volume previously appeared, a few in different versions: *American
Poetry Review, Chariton Review, Cornfield Review, Crazyhorse, Georgia Review,
Hampden-Sydney Poetry Review, Missouri Review, MSS, Negative Capability, New
England Review, New Orleans Review, Ohio Journal, Poetry, Poetry Northwest,
Ploughshares, Southern Poetry Review,* and *Southern Review.* Some of these poems are
included on the recording entitled *Poems of Miller Williams,* #1160, Spoken Arts,
Inc., 1982.
"Inference" and "People" were published as a broadside by Palaemon Press, Ltd.

LIBRARY OF CONGRESS CATALOGING IN PUBLICATION DATA
Williams, Miller.
   The boys on their bony mules.
   I. Title.
PS3545.I53352B6 1983   811'.54   83–905
ISBN 0–8071–1087–6
ISBN 0–8071–1088–4 (pbk.)

FOR JIM AND FOR TOM T.

Contents

The Boys on Their Bony Mules

The Firebreathers at the Café Deux Magots

We sit at a sidewalk table.
Noilly Prat over ice.

A firebreather lost out of time,
his cheeks full of shadows,
takes off his shirt,
starts to spin it like a bullfighter's cape
and drops it.
He opens a blue plastic bottle,
soaks a torch, a broomstick wrapped in rags,
and waves the fire in front of him like a flag.

He seems to drink the alcohol like water.
He breathes in slowly.
He exhales a burning breath
red with yellow borders.

Flames run like liquid.
They drop in brief blazes from chin to chest.

With uncooperative hands and locked-in legs
he does this for nine silent minutes.
He bows like Pinocchio to the proper applause.
Aggressively among us he collects his coins.
His eyes when they come close
are bleary and small.
He seems to be drunk.
His hair is seared away.
His eyes don't have any lashes.
Blisters have shrunk into scars
on his chest and chin
like some exotic fruit left in the field.

One eye seems to be hunting
for something on its own.

He puts the plastic bottle
the torch and the cash
into a canvas bag and wanders away.
His feet sound like gravel poured on the pavement.

A woman plays a flute.
Her tall companion
long breasts moving like lovers
inside her blouse
comes and demands our money with great hands.

Another man,
years younger,
his green eyes lifting like fingers
the faces of women,
sheds his open shirt.

His chest is perfect and hard
and clean as marble.

Over the left nipple
one small round scar.

He opens the plastic bottle. He grins.
He tosses back the hair falling into his eyes
and then he makes a small move with his head,
a small, unconscious move,
the way one turns for a moment in mid-sentence
hearing a tumbler break in another room.

Lost in Ladispoli
for Ruth

Though we may never be seen alive again
by anyone who speaks English well
surely we are somewhere in Italy still
surely we are near the Mediterranean coast moving
by some definition
in this street-wise but halfhearted collapsible Fiat
through rutted mud between these narrow houses.

What the hell way is west?
They'll find us rusted shut, down a dead-end alley,
sitting up and obviously screaming at the end
like the people of Pompeii.

When suddenly here on a building
made from this mud
on a low flat roof a girl
Who knows with these Italians?
seventeen
tall in the warm morning sun in a blue bikini so brief
it barely repeats her mouth, her low-lidded eyes,
brushing out the long, the luminous hair.

She is more Roman this girl than all of Rome.

Her body turns as if the world were turning
(Sweet Love, how like you this?)
slowly as the Fiat fumbles
churning the mud.

She raises an arm.
She may be stretching loose from the last threads of sleep.
She seems to be pointing to something.

3

We take the lane she shows us or seems to show us.

She gazes at us moving toward the sea
as if she has seen something remarkable
something that ought to be precisely remembered.
We stop and look back.
We gather her in
against the pull of gravity
and time
because
she has not yet heard
of either one.

4

Uneasy a February afternoon
we rode the Indian air Calcutta to Delhi.
I leaned across and we looked out the window.
We saw a piece of Nepal, a perfect map.
Beyond Nepal half of the Himalayas
rose past all metaphor. A pot mender
looked up from his work to find us, shading his eyes.
"Look," you said. "There—the man looking up."
But we could not even see the sheep being driven
as slowly as always in front of the pot mender's tent
by his lazy brother-in-law who would certainly lose one
before a year was out to the ravenous wolves.

Aesthetic Distance

The moon is dark. We have our drinks on a terrace
on Gianicolo hill. There is a little war
in the streets of Rome. We see the flashes from pistols,
the sweeping lights, we hear the pistols popping.
We watch a Molotov cocktail burning its curve.
"Star bright," somebody says. "You can make a wish."
I think of another time, on the Gulf Coast.
Standing among the beer cans and towels on the sand,
we watched a tall-masted sailing ship go wrong.
There may have been scratching and prayers, heroic gestures,
while it was sliding out of the bird-ridden air
into the heavy, green, unbreatheable water.
All we knew was the slow glory of its going,
the flapping of sharp flags, the bow in the air,
white against blue, the pause, the empty horizon.

The people filling the street
slide past the fenders of the car
and close in behind us,
eyes at the windows paying no attention
as if we were chugging along in a motor launch
up a river clogged with floating bodies.

No danger here, the driver says. No danger.

Rickshaw drivers don't have any shadows.
The sun falls through them onto the broken pavement.

A dog with no skin stands with stiff legs and trembles.

A woman washing her hair in the running gutter
raises her head for something that floats by.

A bride sits hard in the back of a black Buick
between solemn men like brothers.
Out of a nostril hangs a string of pearls.

The honking rises
one endless syllable
hosannah.

I think of an apple.

A one-legged boy in short black pants
hops out of an alley
as if all of us were cripples
dragging our second legs.

I think of an apple.

Two men who may be students

one wearing only a shirt
one wearing only the pants that belong to the shirt
make their almost unnoticed way
across the street,
their arms moving in quick, important ways.

The later babies, they take a hand or foot.
The driver tells me this. They beg better.
I know the driver is telling me driver's lies.
I pretend to believe him.
I frown. I shake my head.

Gray rags around her bones
a little girl crying
begins to balance her way along a rope
four feet above a clot of uncertain faces.
A woman
moves among the hands
collecting coins.

Barely above the heads
a dead man is borne on a board
riding the high hands of seven men.
He seems to be a narrow raft
down the same thick river.

I think of a single apple, dark,
with pale yellow markings around the stem,
resting in the middle of a small, round, walnut table.
A slender woman wearing a white dress,
touching the table lightly
with her long left hand

stands still and looks at the apple.
There is not a sound
except for one white curtain barely moved by the wind.

Normandy Beach

The waves on the Normandy coast jump heavily toward us.
Somewhere above the rolling, ocean-thick air
soldiers are lining up in a rising light.
The name we have come to find is whitely there.

We stand awhile above the ragged beach
where the German gunnery crews held hard
and spread the beach with bodies that still sprawl,
appearing and disappearing. A silent charge

comes out of the lifting fog, vague visions of men,
some of them drowning, some digging holes in the sand,
some lying on the sand with waves washing their boots.
We watch as the bodies fade away in the sun.

We find his name, Lieutenant, Arkansas.
To leave you there alone I turn around
to a curving monument, The Spirit of Youth
Rising Out of the Sea, what might be found

as frontispiece in a book of Romantic verse.
It must have suggested solace to someone:
arms that might be wings, and flowering waves,
what Shelley as a sculptor might have done.

I watch the statue standing over the stones
and think of what the living do to the dead.
Then suddenly what you came to do is done.
We stop in a dark store for cheese and bread

and a bottle of wine. We find that famous room
where tapestry runs like a frozen picture show

the slow invasion that went the other way
over eleven hundred years ago,

princes and knights and horses in feathers and metal
changing the names of things. An iron cross
leans from an iron gate at the foot of a hill
where careful Germans step out of a touring bus.

I don't want to make a bad metaphor here
and everything is suddenly metaphor.
We head the Fiat south in a sundown light
and follow the back roads. Beside a river

we make the wine outlast the food and sit still
and watch the water run. Thought after thought
comes into my head and goes. Lonely companion,
there's something I have to tell you but I don't know what.

Wiedersehen

When open trucks with German prisoners in them
passed in convoy through the small town
I dreamed in, my fourteenth year, of touchable breasts
and cars and the Cards and the Browns, we grabbed the shirts
we twisted and tied for bases and chased the trucks
past all our houses slow as we could run.

We tossed the baseball up to one of the guards
who sometimes pretended to keep it but threw it back.
Once I threw it badly. A German caught it.
A boy barely older than I was and blonder
and nearly as thin. He grinned and I thought how much
the baseball belonging to John Oscar Carpenter
must have cost. The guard didn't seem concerned
about the baseball or me. We ran for blocks
behind the flatbed truck. The side rails rattling
made the same sense the Germans did
calling and tossing the ball to one another.

We ran in silence needing our breath to breathe
and knowing that begging raises the value of things.
At the edge of town the convoy speeded up.
Everyone stopped but me and the truck pulled away.
I looked back once to see the seven others
standing on the curb of the last street
loose and surprised as a group on a picnic
looking into a river where someone has drowned.

When I turned back to the trucks, pumping my arms,
the pain in my side coming to punish me hard,
to burn the blame away and make us even,

even John Oscar Carpenter and I,
the young German hauled back and let the ball
fly in a flat arc from center field.
I caught it. I held it in the hand I waved
as truck by truck the convoy shifted gears.
"Wiedersehen," he yelled. A word I knew.
I turned and pegged the ball to home in time.
I wondered if he had killed the Rogers boy
or thrown the hand grenade at Luther Tackett
that blew his arm away. I had done something
nobody ever had done. It was large and frightful.
We walked in amazement a while and went to our houses.

Your grandchildren, German, do they believe the story,
the boy in Arkansas, blonder than you?

For Victor Jara
Mutilated and Murdered
The Soccer Stadium
Santiago, Chile

This is to say we remember. Not that remembering saves us.
Not that remembering brings anything usable back.

This is to say that we never have understood how to say this.
Out of our long unbelief what do we say to belief?

Nobody wants you to be there asking the question you ask us.
There had been others before, people who stayed to the end:

Utah and Boston and Memphis, Newgate, Geneva, Morelos—
Changing the sounds of those names, they have embarrassed
    us, too.

What shall we do with the stillness, do with the hate and the
    pity?
What shall we do with the love? What shall we do with the
    grief?

Such are the things that we think of, far from the thought that
    you hung there,
Silver inside of our heads, golden inside of our heads:

Would we have stayed to an end or would we have folded our
    faces?
Awful and awful. Good Friend. You have embarrassed our
    hearts.

The Muse

Driving south on U.S. 71
Forty miles from Fort Smith
I heard a woman speak from the back seat.
"You want a good idea for a closing line?"
I recognized the voice.
"Where did you come from?"
"I wiggled in back there when you stopped for gas.
You'd better pull over."
She knew about the cards I kept in my pocket
to scribble on whenever she came around.
We'd been through this before.
I bumped down from the blacktop and stopped the car.
Between a couple of oaks and a yellow line,
above the howl and sizzle of passing traffic,
she said some words. I waited. She looked out the window.
"Well?", I said. "Is that it?"
"It's all I have," she said. "Can't you do
anything for yourself?"
"I listen," I said. "That's what I'm supposed to do."
She took a slow breath and got out of the car.
"I'll try to get you something.
I'm going to walk around for a little while.
If you leave me here I'll forget I ever saw you."
"I won't leave you," I said. So I'm sitting here
between the darkening road and pin oak trees,
a 3 × 5 card in one hand, a pen in the other,
beginning to feel vulnerable and foolish
like a man waiting for more toilet paper
thinking he may have been left there and forgotten.

Learning to Read

When I suspect I'm a character in a novel—
it's not all the time; Monday morning, for instance,
it's ten o'clock and people are wanting coffee
or I've been waiting a little too long for something,
a dentist, a beer, a bus, a good man's death.
I'm pretty sure I'm real; I buy the whole
ball as they say of wax—
When I suspect I'm being written is mostly
after dinner, the dark sun slipping away.
I'm sitting beside a window watching the sparrows
or watching the dogs tumble through the leaves
or the falling snow.
There's evidence enough, if you think about it:
the pride, the mounting tension,
the recognitions, an hour too late and useless,
the quick turns, the fortunate meetings,
the falling away of enemies and friends,
the obligatory scenes, the ritual candles
we throw before us against the resolving dark.

A Short Play

There is nothing to do for the fact that wraps around her.
She stands at the kitchen window.
She presses her palms against the cold window.

She conjures the mind of a man,
the one who loves her.
She sees herself across a furious street,
waving awhile then standing still and awkward.
She sees her face falling away,
the fingers curling.
The cars are gone. There is only a noisy wind.
A flickering patch of color. A piece of cloth.

This is not good, she says. It is less than enough.

She takes a sheet of paper. She prints her name.
She looks around the room, around the house.
Where will he look?
What book will he read?
She doesn't know where to put it.

The soup. She puts it in the soup.
He comes kissing her home and she serves him the soup.

Now am I happy, she says, then common sense
comes tumbling out of the ceiling.
She thinks about the sloshing in the stomach.
She knows the letters of her name are lost.
This is conveyed by the way one hand
takes slowly hold of the other
and the introduction of blue in the main lights.

Tell me this moment, she says, you love me forever.

I do, he says. This moment I love you forever,
This is guile, she says, Sir, is it not?

Have you been reading Hardy?

Sir, I have.

Then you must understand how things can change.

But will you remember me a little while,
more than a piece of color, a patch of cloth?

We'll miss you greatly, yes, and speak of you often,
as you've heard others often spoken of.
There will be things around the house to remind us.

At this moment the curtain starts to fall.
Four feet from the stage it sticks.
Here we see the legs and feet of the actors
shifting nervously, turning and turning back,
uncertain how to leave the scene
without unwanted laughter, if not with grace.

The Story of a Memory and His Man

There he saw himself across the room,
barely at first as thin as cellophane
sitting in the chair that he had sat in,
holding the stem of the glass that he had held.
He saw his shape take substance, bend the light,
become too thick almost to see through.
He saw the form do things that he had done
twenty minutes ago. Now this can happen.

He felt color falling through his fingers.
He knew that sitting there across the room
he saw the simple memory of himself
collecting the will to be the one to be,
so then the man that used to be the man
would be an image waiting up ahead,
a thin anticipation for a while
and then be nothing. So this is what he did.

He watched until the memory, now a man
with clothes almost the color of his own,
sat down as he, the man himself, had sat
twenty minutes ago. Now this can happen.

Pretending toward the kitchen, past the chair,
he sat himself into his seated self.
He felt the man who was the memory move
and try to cross his legs the other way
to cross him up, he felt a force of will,
then he became congruent with himself,
and wasn't certain whether he had won
or lost and never felt the small reversal,

if he had become the memory of himself,
if he will do forever what was done
twenty minutes ago, will run behind,
will be already dead and lie for twenty
minutes getting cold before he dies.
Or say the memory will never die.
Oh no the memory will never die.
How lucky then how lucky then how lucky.

We

We are pleased now to present for your listening pleasure
This is Civil Defense for your own good.
Stay in your houses. This is not a test.
Something is moving barely above the trees
at the edge of the city coming in from the south.
Stay away from the windows. Turn off all lights.
If you have been caught in your car pull over and stop.
Tons of darkness are falling out of its eyes.
Trees and parts of houses come tumbling out.
From every hole something resembling something
dribbles down. It glistens on the grass.
It has a certain cast. It smells like something. . . .
It's one of ours, it's one of ours. It's all right.
The Second Piano Concerto in B flat.

The Story

In a small town in the mountains they tell of a man
who started showing up in pictures of weddings,
of softball teams and picnics, a dozen years
after he was sealed and weighted down
by a quarter-ton of dry mountain dirt.
His friends were Christian people full of faith.
Some took his face at first as an omen of evil,
some as a sign of favor. When nothing happened
of any special sort in a couple of years
it came to be seen as more a rude intrusion,
something they had to learn to live with
like the smell of the paper mill.
                    It was commonly held
that he was haunting the town for private reasons.
Not knowing where those reasons were like to take him,
some people started undressing in the dark.
Twice the town council in something like secret
hired men who said they could make him go away.

One built a fire and burned hair from the barber shop.
One threw the preacher's cat off the Baptist Church.
When pictures of these events came out in the paper,
the dead man was there in the crowd, watching with wide
    eyes.

Then one day in a shot of a prize hog
at the county fair, five years from the first appearance,
he wasn't there. Some said the burning hair
had worked exceeding slow; some said, the prayers;
some said the cries of the cat had finally done it.

Lovers began to look at each other again;
women took their magazines back to the bathroom.
People wondered what made him go away
as much as they wondered once what brought him back.
The only people who did not seem concerned
were Mary Sue Tattersall and her husband Edward
who ran the seed store at the edge of town,
kept two cows and some chickens, went to bed early,
and Saturday mornings took long walks in the woods.

Rubaiyat for Sue Ella Tucker

Sue Ella Tucker was barely in her teens.
She often minded her mother. She didn't know beans
About what boys can do. She laughed like air.
Already the word was crawling up her jeans.

Haskell Trahan took her for a ride
Upon his motorbike. The countryside
Was wet and beautiful and so were they.
He didn't think she'd let him but he tried.

They rode along the levee where they hid
To kiss a little while and then he slid
His hand inside her panties. Lord lord.
She didn't mean to let him but she did.

And then she thought that she would go to hell
For having let befall her what befell,
More for having thought it rather nice.
And she was sure that everyone could tell.

Sunday morning sitting in the pew
She prayed to know whatever she should do
If Haskell Trahan who she figured would
Should take her out again and ask her to.

For though she meant to do as she was told
His hands were warmer than the pew was cold
And she was mindful of him who construed
A new communion sweeter than the old.

Then sure enough, no matter she would try
To turn her head away and start to cry,

He had four times before the week was out
All of her clothes and all his too awry.

By then she'd come to see how she had learned
As women will a lesson often earned:
Sweet leads to sweeter. As a matter of fact,
By then she was not overly concerned.

Then in the fullness of time it came to be
That she was full of child and Haskell he
Was not to be found. She took herself away
To Kansas City, Kansas. Fiddle-de-dee.

Fiddle-de-dee, she said. So this is what
My mother meant. So this is what I got
For all my love and whispers. Even now
He's lying on the levee, like as not.

She had the baby and then she went to the place
She heard he might be at. She had the grace
To whisper who she was before she blew
The satisfied expression from his face.

The baby's name was Trahan. He learned to tell
How sad his daddy's death was. She cast a spell
Telling how it happened. She left out
A large part of the story but told it well.

Rebecca at Play

She lies in the grass and spreads her golden hair
across the grass, as if for simple joy
in being what she is, quietly aware
that she is not a tree or horse or boy.

Rock

For two days I have dug around a rock
that may have been buried where it was
to hold the county in place.

I am building in front of my house
a wall of fieldstones.

Every two hours I say
I have earned a beer.

All of this afternoon
I have rolled this barely
round and enormous rock
up a gradual hill
to a place prepared
in my lonely and useless wall.

Four times the rock has pulled away
out of the crying grip of my arms and knees
and rolled back to the hole it lay in forever.

I know enough to know when to feel important.

I try to give my mind to something else.
I imagine I may be forgiven for living in town
with two dogs that don't know how to hunt
because this hurts like manhood and my hand is bleeding.

I stop and look at the blood.

I try to give my mind to something else.

It's you and I against the world my love.
The world is

I have to tell you
a prohibitive favorite.

Up there is a fence with a hole the size of this stone.
Here is a house where I live with a better woman
than I had meant to be with and two dumb dogs.

I have earned more beers than I can drink.

The woman across the street
will be naked tonight
stepping out of the bathtub
reaching for something.

My knees are gone.

It's getting late she says.
You ought to come in.

I guess I should I say but look at the rock.

It really is big she says. I don't see how you did it.

Sisyphus my friend
what does forever mean?

I go into the house. She hands me a mug of beer.

Here, unlike forever, it is six o'clock.
The big hand and the little hand, they tell us.

Going

The afternoon in my brother's backyard
when my mother in awful age and failing
in body not at all and twice the pity
thought I was my dead father home for dinner
I didn't know what to tell her. What could I say?
Here I am home Darling give me your hand?
Let us walk together a little while?
Here it is 1915, we are married,
the first of our children is not yet born or buried,
the war in Europe is not yet out of hand
and the one you will not forget who wanted you first
is just as we are, neither old nor dead.
He still frets about us being together.

Good woman wife with five good children to mourn for,
and children arriving with children, what can I say?

See we have come because we wanted to come.
Because of love. Because of bad dreams.
This is my wife. We live in another state.

Trying

The husband and wife had planned it for a long time.
The message was folded into a paper boat.
The children were all asleep. In the backyard
they put the boat in the pool. *We are here. Save us.*

Logos

This is not the place I would like to start
but this is where I am.
Here are hats and horns and the names of states on sticks.
The speaker is spreading out the syllables
of blessings, curses, lies and incantations.
Only the lies are what they pretend to be.

Some words, put to such a use, fare badly.
They change colors. They take on mutant shapes.
They come like a pestilence flapping around the room.
Silently, one by one, they fall to the floor.
One with a tentacle, vermilion and mottled with yellow,
tries to attract my attention. I ignore it to death.

Words when they fall are like the falling of angels.
Words when they die are like the burning of feathers.
They peep like bats.

In the beginning that unbroken breath
the endless exhalation
was broken by the terrible mercy
of God's own tongue, God's teeth,
into one round verb.
Its offspring number so many
nobody could count them.

Words are shadows, words are only shadows.
We take them for more than shadows. They seem to be more.
They enlist in the armies of our poems.
They quiet unhappy lovers and name our children.
They join all things together and put them asunder.
They never hear themselves. They have no ears.

People send them out with clear directions,
Mean this, Mean that.
They undo whatever they do as soon as they do it.
A person would think we might have had enough.
Hush.

I press the silver box I have in my hand.

A jazz quintet is reinventing music.
They play with calm and perfect concentration.
There are no presidents or words in the world.
My floor is as clean as Eden.
As if by a word of God,
Let there not be words,
Let there be a magnificent moving of fingers,
Let there be reeds and brass,
Let there be piano, bass and drum.
Da-biddely-biddely-biddely-biddely-
Bump.

Ah, but we know, don't we?
A waiter can hear you make that sound all day
and he never will bring you a cheese sandwich
no matter how badly you want one.

In the beginning was F sharp.

That would have been a very different story.

is trying to find a way to get out of town.
The people are running at him from all directions.

The woman who believed in two is dead
in the automatic door at the supermarket.

The girl who wrote the report on the power of four
is naked and tied to the door in the teachers' lounge.

The boy who turned his parents in for saying
one and six before supper has hanged himself.

Triplets are holy. A three-base hit is holy.
Tricorn hats are back in style again.
Trivia has come into its own. Think of a question.

Children's Games

When the music is going strong
and everybody is marching along
you can bet he has put in his grey
hand and jerked a chair away.

He counts to seventy-five,
Oh, Love, if he plays fair,
but you can't take your time;
he may not go that far.

And when he lifts his head
and turns from side to side
he'll see our shirt tails flapping
no matter where we hide.

Somebody leaves. You wonder where he goes.
The bottle spins and wobbles and comes to rest
pointing toward somebody on your right.
You grin inside yourself and feel blessed.
Now again the bottle spins and slows.

The blind man gropes and our feet are frozen.
We lean away. We are not chosen,
We are stumbled on. How would it be
worse or better if he could see?

Learning

You sit by the bed
holding one of the disinterested hands.
You feel it lose its resistance.
It begins to cool.
Someone comes in and puts a hand on your shoulder.
You go home and make coffee.
You start to take off your clothes and you fall asleep.
The cup of coffee gets cold on the kitchen table.

His eyes shine like an expensive car.
His voice is distant and clear, like the Greek Islands. We move
around him as if someone were writing his name
all the time.
He forgives us our excessive love.

We do need the great ones, who brush their teeth
and never spit and who it hurts to think of
ever picking their noses, who have good breath.

O they are important for looking down as they do.
It is not true
that in the bathroom they act like anyone else.
They act great.

Still we know, we know,
for every object of universal acclaim
there must be someone highly respected and fussy
who never heard the name
and snorts and grumbles when he tells us so.

People

When people are born
we lift them like little heroes
as if what they have done
is a thing to be proud of.

When people die
we cover their faces
as if dying were something
to be ashamed of.

Of shameful and varied heroic things we do
except for the starting and stopping
we are never convinced
of how we feel.
We say oh, and well.

Ah, but in the beginning
and in the end.

A Newspaper Picture of Spectators at a Hotel Fire

At three in the afternoon on a clear day
fire breaks out in a tall St. Louis hotel
on the 16th floor and takes it from end to end.

That is how high above this street of faces
as fixed as stones three women stood in windows
with cracking glass behind them till one by one
they tested the air like swimmers and stepped stiffly out.
They come down with zeroes in their mouths.

One among the watchers has turned his back
on such important people who step into nothing,
who kick their way to the curb, to the tops of cars.
He takes away what he wants, the negative faces.

All morning we are moody. We mention the picture,
the long, slow arms, the women falling toward us.

Inference

The mouse
curling fur wet and warm
inside the belly of the owl
has been we might say born backward out of his life.

There is a man then who talks backward.
I mean he walks down the street moving his lips
and syllables fly into his mouth.
He could unsay die and the dead would rise,
day and the sun would go down.

Here though he has moved his mouth
and we are undone and distant,
love and touch
curled up and moist
in the little sacs of his lungs.

Because it was time to sit we sat together.
We talked until the air
aged into evening, shade by solvent shade,
until we looked and there was nothing there.
We were not old enough to be afraid

and so we sat still in the dark and talked of truth
and true faith and doubt
and all our obligations to the dead,
and what death means, and life. Then she came out
and turned on the light and sat down. "Listen," she said,

"western philosophy is camel shit
and mysticism is worse.
The desert gods all want in our underwear.
To make a garden and love and a small verse
will serve us for works. And even faith. And prayer.

The truth is gone. Go weed and prune and hoe
and keep the rabbits away;
invite somebody to bed and try to be friends;
write some of it out to see what you meant to say.
All of the other means will marry their ends."

We didn't argue with her; she seemed so certain
of what she believed, while we
were certain of nothing. Now she's equally sure
the Blood of the Lamb alone will set her free.
She climbed around us and left us where we were.

We had seemed, beside her, like people of faith.
Now we seemed consigned

to outer darkness. As in a mystic riddle,
not moving we move from right to left, to find
we're still alone in our own excluded middle.

Our minds, still un-made-up like unmade beds,
may by their convolutions
catch us unawares; a sudden burning
may have us mid-sentence taking new positions,
pleasuring ourselves on any startled morning.

Paying Some Slight Attention to His Birthday
the Associate Professor Goes About His Business
Considering What He Sees and a Kind of Praise

Standing in front of my students,
a careful man,
I hear one tumbler turn.

The students are sitting still in their one-armed chairs
like rows of slot machines,
most surely come to rest
on the wrong combinations.

I have not helped them very much.

I love them. I tell them the truth:

The underside of the soul is rough to the touch.

The smell of the armpits of angels
is like the sound of tomatoes,
the falling of pickles.

It's easier to find the smallest needle
than prove there's not one hidden in the haystack.

For a sonnet you put two limericks together
and one verse of The Old Rugged Cross.

Now it is suppertime. I have done my job.

The sun coming down makes me feel sad and contented,
like finding the house of your life ten years ago,
another car in the driveway,
the crepe myrtle gone.

A dog drops at my feet again and again
a rubber ball to be thrown across the grass.

All of my children have loved me
more than they might have
and in their own skins do love me still.

Across the road a cow
settles into the grass
or the sun
settles into the grass like a casual cow,
slow and heavy and full to its simple face
with the unquestionable rightness of being a cow
or the sun
whichever it is going down into the grass
this suddenly silent hour, this year come round.

In Nashville, Standing in the Wooden Circle Sawed Out from the Old Ryman Stage, the Picker Has a Vision
for Tom T.

I'll tell you what it was. I thought about those
who suddenly came on lines they couldn't cross over—
Hank and Patsy and Hawkshaw and Gentleman Jim
and all the others who did what they did and are gone.
John Keats and Wilfred Owen and Jimmie Rodgers.

Standing a misplaced man in that crowded space
with nobody breathing but me, I had nothing to say.
My head was full of words from those good pickers
about our lives and the lives they take us to.
Lord, the years of wine and city lights.

I thought of the small square of the planet earth
I say I own, of my ridiculous self
pacing it off drunk at four in the morning
trying to understand what a place is worth.

It's a long time gone that we stopped counting things;
neither of us is going to die young.
Still fish grow fat, they lay their eternal eggs,
full grow the breasts and long the slender legs
of the young women we watch and forget about.

I heard it said by a woman in full sun
who only tells her lies from dusk till dawn
that nothing guards heaven or hell; it's the days to come
in this plain world without us we can't get through to.

I tell you, Tom, they will not let us pass.
Madness, Old Age and Death, the rough boys
who come down from the hills on bony mules

know where we mean to go and they mean to stop us.
They make a line in the dirt and stand there.
Madness we can deal with. We know his moves.
And Death's a sissy; he never comes full face
when he's all by himself. He sneaks about. He hides.
Old Age is slow but he never stops to rest.
He can chase us down like a schoolyard bully
and sit on our chests until we barely breathe
while Death creeps close to put out his fist and hit us.

So what do we do, Tom? I'll tell you what.
We take our breaths and loves to let them go
and tell the names of things to the forgetful air.

Sir

(One of the President's people has something to say
January 20, 1981)

In the first world we know there is only the present.
Nothing was or will be. Then only the future.
Then only the past, and then we are the past.

This we understand is the nature of things.

Still, when Time falls in to fill the places
our unaccountable hands have hollowed out,
we, being who we are, will flail against it
because we have not done what we meant to do,
because there has not been much that we understood
and the little we learned returned us to where we started.

This may also be in the nature of things.

We have dreamed of honor and the forthright heart
as persons blind from birth imagine light,
have barely begun to find the uses of love,
have learned to speak of that giving and greedy god
who is the earth and will not forgive us always,
into whose mouths we have lowered our fathers and mothers
and children forever. He is jealous and knows our names.

History stands, like a sad teacher, beside us,
waiting to lay a ruler across our backs
to say again that we have answered wrongly.

What we wanted to do we have not done
but we have done a hard thing to do.
Love (this most worn word) we have not understood;
on rare days, even so, we have used it well.

What we wanted to do we have not done
but we have done the longest thing to do.

This is not to commemorate an end.

What have we done? Sir, we have done right.
Right once done, there is no ending to it.

Letters

For WW

It's strange to read the words of a dead friend
when word of his death has not outrun his letter.
To learn that you have written him in turn
days after he was dead, asking his plans,
is strange. You understand the cartoon dog
who finds he's overshot the edge of the cliff
so stands on nothing and, seeing the fact, falls.

Or say I felt I'd walked into a door
I thought was open. Embarrassed I wanted to know
what passing brat had shut that heavy door.

It wasn't as if I could knock and it would open.

Opening words of letters I meant to write
are falling out of the mailbox, Dear Friend, Dear Friend.

The dramatic pause. The bump under the wheel.
The woman in Greece, how beautiful she was.
Try to avoid the only subject there is.
Still there's no point in lying. All of us live here.
Anyone not afraid of the dark is a fool.
Jesus why do we keep on doing this?

Birth of the Blues

John Keats never read Dylan Thomas or Yeats.
Dante didn't know Shakespeare. Neither did Jesus.
I think of those I will never know, from countries
whose languages sound to me like mathematics,
that prince, for instance, who wrote in Siamese
in the seventeenth century, who could well have been
the best of all of us for all I know.

I think about that poet born today
in Montreal whose verses will go with vessels
blown by the lights of stars to the curling edge.

I know he is there. Listen. This is the time.
Or she is. Lord. Lord. I feel like Herod.

Running into Things
for twelve in their pickup trucks

As lemmings run into the sea, old priests appear
at the house of Thomas Aquinas and Thomas More
to fix their faith and Hume opens the door.
They ran that way before the sea was there.

Because they couldn't remember the bypass
that cut across their roads and cut them down
a dozen farmers have died coming to town.
All they remembered was dust, gravel and grass.

Documenting It

First he could not remember
where T. S. Eliot said
"Between the plan and the act falls the shadow"
or if what he said was plan or something else.
This bothered him so that he thought of cutting back
to one or two martinis after supper.

Second he forgot
why he had driven down to the grocery store.
He sat in the parking lot for ten minutes.
Why did I drive down to the grocery store?
He went home and fixed himself a drink
and waited for his wife to ask where the soap was.

Third he could not remember
what class he was teaching,
Comparative Physiology, Biology I,
or something he had forgotten how to do.
He thought of those dreams of final examinations
in classes he registered for but never attended,
meant to but never did, couldn't find out
where it was meeting until the day of finals.
He had to go and look at the awful questions.

He found that when he panicked he was aroused.
He thought this might be worth a minor paper.

He prayed but it did not help. It does not always.

The Young Lt. Col.

The young Lt. Col. planning his coup;
the preacher like an eternal teacher's pet
describing our punishment, saying you'd better not;
the one who decorates the toilet walls;
those who build bridges or blow them down;
the one who tells a scene he never saw
remembering things not as they were at all—
these are the same person. Well, aren't they? Aren't they?

Some Lines Finished Just Before Dawn
at the Bedside of a Dying Student
It Has Snowed All Night

The blind from birth, they do not know
that roads diminish as they go
away from us. They know that in
our later years the hair grows thin.
They know it sometimes goes away.
They do not know it turns to gray.
They do not know what mirrors are.
They do not comprehend the dark
any better than the light.
They may recognize the night
as chill and a change in how things sound
and how we gather inside the house.
They do not know the way they cast
their morning shadows toward the west.
They have to trust that moon and star
are something as we say they are.
They cannot know with certainty,
whatever we say, that we can see.

Some physicists believe in four
planes of space. This is more
than we can know, lacking the sense
to see the plane our reason bends
about the other three. This
is not called faith. That's what it is.

Confessing faith, had we as well
let in God and heaven? And hell,
fastened as it is to heaven?
So the soul becomes a given,
given heaven and hell and Him?

And cherubim and seraphim?
Ghosts and ogres? Vampires? Elves?
People who can turn themselves
to cats and make potatoes rot
and curdle a mother's milk? Why not?
This man with tubes is going to die
today, tonight, tomorrow. I,
I, I, I . . . How good
that sounds to me. If I could
would I take his place? I don't
have to answer and I won't.
But I am angry at the snow
caught in the car lights. We don't know,
though we watch him, what he will do,
don't know if he is passing through
a wall or running into one,
to fall together, all of him done.

In either case we say goodbye
mostly with our eyes and try
to be exactly here, to watch
beside him while he dies, with such
an ease it seems we mean to go
beside him all the way. And so
we do. As far as we can see.
That says less than it seems to say.
Already the light when I turn that way
is dim. Sometimes I see the shapes
of people flying. Or clouds, perhaps.
Or trees. Or houses. Or nothing at all.

These are the thin thoughts you call
to the front of my mind. It's a feathery three
o'clock in the morning. We've gotten through
almost another measured night.

There's love to serve and sufficient light
in the living mode. I wish you would stay.

The nurse will disturb you soon. I will say
good morning again. I will mention the snow.
I will lie about this. I will get my coat
and tie my shoes. I will stop and stand
by the bed a while and hold your hand
longer than you like for me to
and drive home dying more slowly than you.

Living on the Surface

The dolphin
walked upon the land a little while
and crawled back to the sea
saying something thereby
about all that we live with.

Some of us
have followed him from time to time.
Most of us stay.
Not that we know what we're doing here.

We do it anyway
lugging a small part of the sea around.
It leaks out our eyes.

We swim inside ourselves
but we walk on the land.

What's wrong, we say, what's wrong?

Think how sadness soaks into
the beds we lie on.

Jesus, we've only just got here.
We try to do what's right
but what do we know?

In Another Town

Out of a sealed window
in a bookless room where I have stayed too long
I see a man and a woman standing on a bridge.
I wonder why they are there this hour of the morning.
They grip the railing.
I suppose they are trying to solve a problem.
They leave without touching and walk in different directions.
Daylight takes over the bridge cable by cable.
If someone were to come now and knock on the door
I would say, "Look how sunlight collects on the bridge."